D0984007

Cockroach

Toney Allman

KIDHAVEN PRESS™

THOMSON™

GALE

San Diego • Detroit • New York • San Francisco • Cleveland
New Haven, Conn. • Waterville, Maine • London • Munich

THOMSON

GALE

Picture Credits

Cover: © Richard T. Nowitz/CORBIS
AP/Wide World Photos, 6, 7
© Anthony Bannister; Gallo Images/CORBIS, 14
© Dee Breger/Photo Researchers, Inc., 4
© John Burbidge/Photo Researchers, Inc., 8 (inset)
COREL Corporation, 20 (bottom), 25 (left)
© Ecoscene/CORBIS, 26
© Gusto/Photo Researchers, Inc., 24
© Catherine Karnow/CORBIS, 27
© Ken Lucas/Visuals Unlimited, 15, 18, 22
PhotoDisc/KidHaven Press, 9
© Robert Pickett/CORBIS, 17
© Dr. Morley Read/Photo Researchers, Inc., 12
© Reuters/NewMedia/CORBIS, 21
© Richard Seaman/KidHaven Press, 8, 19, 25 (right)
© Science VU/Visuals Unlimited, 13
© Barbara Strnadova/ Photo Researchers, Inc., 10
© B.G. Thomson/Photo Researches, Inc., 2

For more information, contact
KidHaven Press
27500 Drake Rd.
Farmington Hills, MI 48331-3535
Or you can visit our Internet site at http://www.gale.com

LIBRARY OF CONGRESS CATALOGING-IN-PUBLICATION DATA

Allman, Toney.
  Cockroach / by Toney L. Allman.
    p. cm.—(Bugs)
  Summary: Describes the physical characteristics, behavior, and habitat of cockroaches.
    ISBN 0-7377-1767-X (alk. paper)
  1.Cockroaches—Juvenile literature. [1. Cockroaches.] I. Title. II. Series.
    QL505.5.A45 2004
    595.7'28—dc21
 	
                                                                                  2003009411

TABLE OF CONTENTS

Chapter 1
What Is a Cockroach?   5

Chapter 2
From Egg to Adult   11

Chapter 3
Wild and Domestic Homes   16

Chapter 4
Struggling to Survive   23

Glossary   29

For Further Exploration   30

Index   32

What Is a Cockroach?

Cockroaches are insects that live everywhere, even at the North and South Poles. There are four thousand kinds of cockroaches in the world—fifty-seven different kinds in America alone. Some, like the German cockroach and American cockroach, are pests that live in people's homes. However, most cockroaches, like the Pennsylvania wood-roach, live in the wild in forests or deserts.

Opposite: Cockroaches are insects that live everywhere, including in people's homes. Here, a cockroach head has been magnified many times its normal size.

5

Some cockroaches, like these Madagascar hissing cockroaches, grow to be several inches long.

From Tiny to Huge

Cockroaches come in all different sizes. German cockroaches are almost an inch long. American cockroaches are about an inch and a half long. The smallest cockroach in the world, the wild guest cockroach, is only one-eighth of an inch long. It is so tiny that it lives comfortably in ants' nests. The world's largest cockroach, the Australian giant burrowing cockroach, is found in Australia. Unlike most cockroaches it has no wings and is slow moving, but it can grow to be five inches long and weigh an ounce. The Madagascar hissing cockroach, from the island of Madagascar, is big, too. It can be as big as a small mouse.

Different kinds of cockroaches may look different from one another. They may live in different places. Yet all share certain things that make them part of the insect world.

Body Armor

Like all insects, cockroaches do not have skeletons or bones inside their bodies. A cockroach wears its skeleton on the outside. A cockroach has an oval body with a hard covering over it, called an **exoskeleton**. It protects the soft body parts on the inside. Most, but not all, cockroach exoskeletons are brown or black. The green banana cockroach from Cuba, for example, is a beautiful green color.

The Australian giant burrowing cockroach's hard exoskeleton protects the insect's soft body parts.

Under the exoskeleton a cockroach body is divided into three main parts. First is the head. On the head are large eyes and strong jaws. These jaws do not chew up and down. Instead they move from side to side, like scissors. With them the cockroach can bite even very tough foods.

Thorax

The **thorax** is the middle part of the cockroach body. The cockroach's legs and wings attach to the thorax.

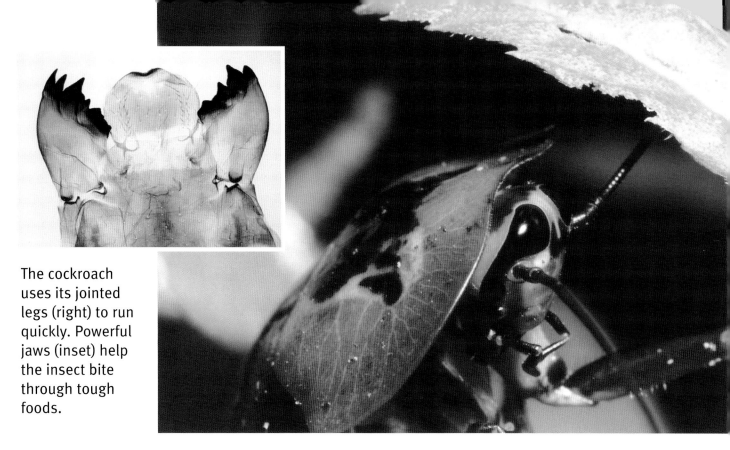

The cockroach uses its jointed legs (right) to run quickly. Powerful jaws (inset) help the insect bite through tough foods.

Like all insects, cockroaches have six legs. The cockroach's legs are long, thin, and **jointed** so that they bend as knees do. They help the cockroach to run very fast. The American cockroach, for instance, can run fifty-nine inches in one second! Most cockroaches have wings, and many are good fliers.

Body of a Cockroach

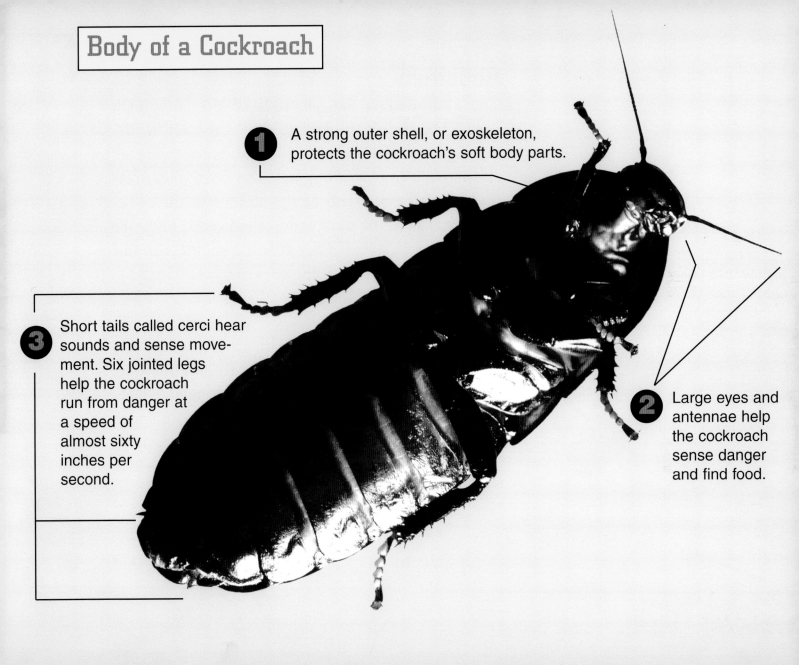

1 A strong outer shell, or exoskeleton, protects the cockroach's soft body parts.

2 Large eyes and antennae help the cockroach sense danger and find food.

3 Short tails called cerci hear sounds and sense movement. Six jointed legs help the cockroach run from danger at a speed of almost sixty inches per second.

Abdomen

The **abdomen** is the last part of the cockroach body. The abdomen is not only a stomach for digesting food. The cockroach also breathes with its abdomen, using breathing holes on both sides of its body. On the rear end of the abdomen, the cockroach has a pair of short tails, called **cerci**. They are the cockroach's ears. They feel the slightest sound or puff of air, and warn the cockroach of danger.

Antennae

A cockroach breathes with its stomach, hears with its cerci, and tastes with its **antennae**. Cockroaches have a pair of long antennae, or feelers, on their heads. These antennae smell and taste the environment, helping the cockroach to find food, sense danger, and recognize other cockroaches.

The cockroach's antennae taste and smell the environment.

From Egg to Adult

Most cockroaches live only a year or two. So new cockroaches must be born often to replace the ones that die. A female cockroach makes eggs as soon as she is an adult. She will do so three or four times during her life.

A female cockroach does not lay her eggs separately, as other insects do. In her abdomen the eggs are enclosed inside a special case that looks like a tiny purse. It is called an **ootheca**. Usually there are a couple of dozen eggs in the ootheca. The average ootheca is less than a half inch long. The female carries the egg case attached to her abdomen, protecting the eggs from danger. When the time nears for the eggs to hatch, the cockroach drops the ootheca in a dark, out-of-the-way place. Now the eggs are on their own.

Cockroach nymphs cling to their mother after hatching.

The Birthday

The eggs hatch and **nymphs** come out of the ootheca. A nymph is a newborn cockroach. It looks like the adult cockroach, except it is smaller, has no wings, and is white. The newly hatched nymphs are hungry. The empty ootheca is their first meal. They are ready to eat and grow. The nymphs search for other food by themselves.

Busting Out

As the cockroach nymph eats, it grows rapidly, but this presents a problem. There is not much room for growing inside a hard exoskeleton. The nymph must **molt** in order to grow. When the nymph becomes too fat for its exoskeleton, it puffs up its body with air. The back of the exoskeleton is broken open. Then out crawls the nymph wearing a new, soft exoskeleton that will harden in a few hours. The nymph is slightly larger than it was before it molted. Over and over, for several months the nymph molts. Finally, after seven or eight molts, when the nymph

A cockroach nymph (pictured) molts seven or eight times before emerging as an adult.

Only a few nymphs survive to become adults in the cockroach world.

crawls out of its old exoskeleton it is not a nymph anymore. It is a fully grown adult cockroach with wings.

Most nymphs, though, do not make it to adulthood. Because they are soft and helpless while molting, they are often attacked and eaten by other animals. Many other nymphs die from starvation or sickness. Only a few grow to be adults in the cockroach world.

A Different Kind of Parent

While most newborn cockroaches must fend for themselves, one kind of cockroach actually protects it young. That is the Australian giant burrowing cockroach, which is quite unusual in the cockroach world. It can live for ten years. It mates and makes eggs about once a year throughout its life. The female carries the ootheca in her abdomen until the eggs hatch. So the nymphs are born alive from her body. Then she cares for them, even bringing them food to eat until they are grown.

Most cockroaches, however, do not live in families. They have to find food and homes as best they can. Yet cockroaches are tough enough that some of them always succeed.

A giant wood cockroach nymph (center) sheds its hard exoskeleton several times before becoming a fully grown cockroach with wings.

Wild and Domestic Homes

Opposite: Domestic cockroaches, like this American cockroach, are common in homes and restaurants.

Most cockroaches do not make homes. They find them. Domestic cockroaches are cockroaches that live around people. Domestic cockroaches find homes inside people's houses. They can live in a beautiful mansion, a small hut, or a neat suburban house. They also live in warehouses, in barns or sheds, and in stores or restaurant kitchens. German

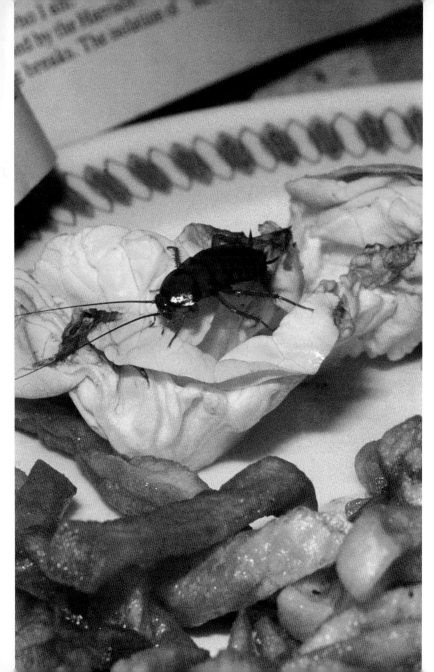

cockroaches are especially satisfied with these places. All a German cockroach needs is a small crack in a wall or floor to make a home. Another domestic cockroach, the American cockroach, likes a wetter environment. It is especially happy in sewers or mines. It also likes the seafaring life. American cockroaches find small cracks for homes on ships and travel all over the world.

A Crack for Everyone

Even though they do not live in families, cockroaches like to live together with other cockroaches. Many domestic cockroaches can crowd into a very small area, as long as each has its own spot in a crack in the wall. A German cockroach can make a home in a crack only one-sixteenth of an inch wide.

Cockroaches hide during the day and eat at night.

Cockroaches are **nocturnal**. They hide in their homes by day and come out to eat and explore at night. During the day the cockroach likes to sit in its crack with its back up against the wall. Its antennae stick out of the crack, waving around and smelling and tasting the environment. As long as it has a little warmth, a crack to hide in, and darkness, a domestic cockroach is comfortable.

Homes in the Wild

Wild cockroaches have very similar needs to domestic cockroaches. They also must find a home that provides warmth, darkness, and a tight place to hide. Wild cockroaches usually live in deserts, in forests, and in warm, tropical places. A wild cockroach is very comfortable in the **leaf litter** on the forest floor. This thick layer of dead and dying leaves and plants makes a perfect cockroach home.

Always there is a little crack in a tree root, a stone with a little hole underneath, or a rotting log or piece of bark where a cockroach can safely hide. In deserts cockroaches find homes under rocks, in caves, or under a pile of brush.

Some wild cockroaches live beside people's homes. The wild smokybrown cockroach, for example, likes woodpiles or cracks on the outside of houses. Some wild cockroaches live with other wild animals. The desert cockroach of Texas sneaks into the burrow homes of wood rats. It makes its home in a crack in the dirt or under the bedding that the wood rat has gathered.

The Digger

The Australian giant burrowing cockroach is different from other cockroaches in many ways. It is the only cockroach that makes a home. It builds a burrow in the sandy soil in

Cockroaches like this one live in leaf litter, caves, and brush.

Thousands of cockroaches, like this
wood cockroach (right), make their
home in a cave.

the wilds of Australia. It digs into the soil with its powerful spiny legs, tossing out the soil with its hard, shovel-shaped head. It makes a deep burrow, sometimes three feet deep, which is the cockroach's permanent, lifetime home. Here the Australian burrowing cockroach finds safety, warmth, and darkness.

All cockroaches use their homes to stay safe. A hole in the ground, a tiny crack in a wall, or a tent of rotting bark provides any cockroach with all the requirements of a perfect home.

The Australian giant burrowing cockroach uses its spiny legs and shovel-shaped head to dig a home in the ground.

Struggling to Survive

Once a cockroach has found a home, it spends most of its life searching for food and trying to avoid danger. Cockroaches are **scavengers**, eating dead plants or animals instead of hunting for themselves. Cockroaches are also **omnivorous**. That means they can eat almost anything, plant or animal.

Opposite: Cockroaches spend most of their lives searching for food.

23

Finding Food

When night falls cockroaches come out of their homes to scavenge for food. They taste and smell with their antennae, searching for anything that might be worth nibbling. Any dead bodies of insects or other animals are eaten. Dead and rotting leaves or plants are also eaten. Domestic cockroaches will actually eat leather, a bar of soap, or the glue on an envelope. It does not take much food to make a meal for a cockroach. One grain of rice can be a satisfying meal.

The Fussy Eater

All cockroaches can eat anything, except the Australian giant burrowing cockroach. It only eats the dead leaves from the Australian eucalyptus tree. Without dry, dead, eucalyptus leaves the Australian giant burrowing cockroach will die of starvation.

Scavenging, whether for dry leaves or dead bodies, can be very dangerous. Cockroaches have many enemies that

A cockroach uses its long antennae to search out its next meal.

24

would like a cockroach meal. Cockroaches have to be alert for danger, ready to dash back into their homes at the first sign of a **predator**. Sometimes even hiding in their homes is not enough.

Attack of the Army Ants

In the tropical forests great columns of army ants live and hunt. For the insects that live on the forest floor, army ants are a terrible danger. The army ants march through the forest, overpowering every insect in their path.

The Australian giant burrowing cockroach (right) eats only dead leaves from the Australian eucalyptus tree (above).

Cockroaches dart into their homes when army ants are on the march, but hiding is useless. Ants on the hunt can easily discover hiding cockroaches. They swarm over the cockroaches, tearing them to pieces.

Some cockroaches try to escape by running up the branches of bushes. The ants follow them. Up, up, to the tips of twigs, the cockroaches run, until they are forced to leap into the jaws of death waiting below.

Some cockroaches try to fly away, but another danger waits. Swarms of birds follow the army ants, looking for just such an opportunity. Any cockroach that flies upward is snatched from the air by a hungry bird.

Enemies Everywhere

Almost any animal will eat a cockroach if it can catch one. Spiders are especially fond of cockroach meals. A particular threat is the spider

A cockroach clings to the rim of an insect-eating pitcher plant.

Many animals, including humans, eat cockroaches. Cockroaches for sale at a market in Thailand are shown here.

known as the giant cockroach hunter. The giant cockroach hunter hides in ambush, waiting for a cockroach to wander by. Then it leaps on the cockroach and quickly injects it with venom. When the cockroach is paralyzed, the spider sucks its victim dry, leaving behind only the empty exoskeleton.

Life is a tough battle for cockroaches, but cockroaches are tough. They have lived on the earth for millions of years, and some of them always survive to scavenge another day.

GLOSSARY

abdomen: The third and last section of the cockroach body.

antennae: Pair of long, thin feelers on the cockroach head, used for sensing, tasting, and smelling the environment.

cerci: A small pair of antenna-like organs on the rear of the cockroach abdomen. They sense sounds and currents of air.

exoskeleton: A skeleton on the outside of the body.

jointed: Formed with joined parts that are able to move and bend.

leaf litter: The layer of dead and rotting material covering the forest floor.

molt: The casting off of the old exoskeleton in order to grow.

nocturnal: Active at night and resting or sleeping by day.

nymph: An immature cockroach without developed wings. The cockroach child.

omnivorous: Eating a wide range of foods, both animals and plants.

ootheca: The purselike egg case, attached to the female cockroach's body, that holds her eggs.

predator: An animal that attacks and feeds on other animals.

scavenger: An animal that feeds on dead plants or animals.

thorax: The middle part of the cockroach body, where the legs and wings are attached.

FOR FURTHER EXPLORATION

Books

Sylvia Branzei, *Grossology Begins at Home,* Reading, MA: Planet Dexter Books, 1997. Read about cockroaches in people's homes and other everyday really gross things. A fun book.

Laurence Pringle, *Cockroaches: Here, There, and Everywhere,* New York: Crowell, 1971. Very interesting descriptions of domestic cockroaches, how they get into people's houses, how they live, and how they have survived.

D.M. Souza, *Insects Around the House.* Minneapolis: Carolrhoda Books, 1991. Learn about the common insects people see close to home, including cockroaches.

Websites

The Madagascar Giant Hissing Cockroach (www.geocities.com/CapeCanaveral/Lab/5466). This site for teachers tells all about how to have a classroom project raising Madagascar hissing cockroaches. Lots of neat pictures and extra sites to look at, too.

Purdue Bug Bowl (http://news.uns.purdue.edu/UNS/bugbowl/bugbowl.index.html). Visit this page from Purdue University to see the crazy insect contests at the students' spring festival every year. There are cockroach races, cricket spitting contests, and foods cooked with insects.

Ralph Online: Giant Cockroaches (www.geocities.com/Research Triangle/5588/roaches.html). Learn all about Australian giant burrowing cockroaches as pets, and listen to the screams!

University of South Carolina Roach Camera (http://cricket.biol.sc.edu/usc-roach-cam.html). The roach camera is turned on the Madagascar hissing cockroaches all the time. Refresh the page to watch what the cockroaches are doing.

Yucky Roach World (http://yucky.kids.discovery.com/flash/roaches). Discover amazing roach facts with your reporter, Wendell Worm.

INDEX

abdomen, 10, 11–12
American cockroaches
  habitat of, 5, 17
  size of, 6
antennae, 10
army ants, 25–26
Australian giant burrowing
  cockroaches
  diet of, 24
  homes of, 19–21
  reproduction and parenting
  by, 15
  size of, 6

cerci, 10
color, 7, 12

desert cockroaches, of Texas,
  10
diet, 18, 23–24
domestic cockroaches,
  16–17

eggs, 11–12
eucalyptus trees, 24
exoskeleton, 6–7, 13–14

food, 18, 23–24

German cockroach
  habitat of, 5, 16–17
  size of, 6
giant cockroach hunters, 28
green banana cockroaches, 7

habitats, 5
  of domestic cockroaches,
  16–17
  of wild cockroaches, 18–19
hearing, sense of, 10
homes
  of domestic cockroaches,
  17
  of wild cockroaches, 18–19

jaws, 7

legs, 7–8, 21
life span, 11, 15

Madagascar hissing
  cockroaches, 6
molting, 13–14

nocturnal habits, 18
nymphs
  appearance of, 12
  molting of, 13–14
  survival of, 14–15

ootheca, 12

Pennsylvania woodroaches, 5
predators, 25–26, 28

reproduction, 11–12, 15

scavenging, 23
sizes, 6
smell, sense of, 10
speed, 8
spiders, 26, 28
stomach, 10

taste, sense of, 10
thorax, 7–8

wild smoky brown
  cockroaches, 10
wings, 8, 12